MW01104687

"Jesus Does Stand-Up,"
and Other Satires

To Sean,
with best wishes, Gordon S Jackson

"Jesus Does Stand-Up," and Other Satires

Parables, Pictures, and Parodies for Today's Church

Gordon S Jackson

Gordon S. Jackson

RESOURCE *Publications* • Eugene, Oregon

"JESUS DOES STAND-UP," AND OTHER SATIRES
Parables, Pictures, and Parodies for Today's Church

Resource Publications
An Imprint of Wipf and Stock Publishers
199 W. 8th Ave., Suite 3
Eugene, OR 97401
www.wipfandstock.com

ISBN 13: 978-1-60899-038-2

Manufactured in the U.S.A.

For Dan Vaughan

Contents

Acknowledgments

I AM indebted to various people for their help in bringing this volume to fruition. Foremost among them are my family, Sue, Sarah and Matthew, for their encouragement and especially for their critiques and suggestions.

I am also grateful to the following friends and colleagues for their feedback on drafts of the manuscript: Jim Edwards, Jeff and Beryl Haschick, Dave and Jan Hicks, Jeff O'Connor, Greg Orwig, Fiona Pollifax, Ron Pyle, Colin Storm, Janelle Thayer, Steve Watts, and Ginny Whitehouse.

But more important still is the need to thank those saints who have somehow remained immune to the less-than-Christian conduct or values that are spoofed in this book. These rare individuals provided the motivation for this book by showing the rest of us that we too can live lives worthy of the One who has called us.

Introduction

"They sought the world, and it fled them not."

—JOHN KNOX (1505–1572),
ON CERTAIN PASTORS OF HIS DAY

IF HUMOR, as someone has said, is God's aspirin, then satire must be His penicillin or even steroids: far stronger medicine, to be taken with caution. Satire is a risky business at the best of times. When it dares to tread upon sacred turf, however, that risk increases exponentially.

This book assumes that risk is worth taking, for two reasons. One is that God sometimes uses humor to help His people see their weaknesses and foibles in a way that sermons or Bible studies might not. The second is that at least some Christians have enough of a sense of humor, and are mature enough in their faith, that they're able to risk looking in a mirror—a mirror that won't always yield flattering images.

For instead of being soothingly reader friendly, this collection of parables, pictures and parodies about the contemporary church is meant to be provocative. I expect that some of these pieces will annoy or even anger some readers. To the extent that you respond that way because of my failure to make my point, I'm sorry.

On the other hand, it may be that some pieces in this collection can fill the same corrective or warning role that God provides for his people throughout scripture. At times, such as when Jesus spoke scathingly of the religious authorities of his day, the message was blunt and painful. Thus, as you read the vignettes in this volume, you too may encounter truths that hit closer to home than you like. If, as the saying goes, "the shoe fits," you're invited to take away whatever lessons you can to help you become a more faithful and God-pleasing member of Christ's church. If the shoe doesn't fit, keep trying others. For I suspect that all but the most saintly in our midst have a lesson or two to learn from the ideas presented here. To the extent that we do, we will be asking, in John Knox's words, whether as Christians "we have sought the world and it has fled us not"—and, with that heightened awareness, what God would have us do next. (And in case it isn't apparent from the context, be assured that with rare exceptions all churches, organizations and individuals referred to in these entries are fictitious. The exceptions are obvious historical or living characters, such as Queen Elizabeth II, or organizations like universities that are referred to purely to make a satirical point. Otherwise, any resemblance to real persons or organizations is purely coincidental.)

This book seeks to make two simple yet uncomfortable points. The first is that the Western church, particularly in the United States, lives out its life and calling in an often unfriendly, even hostile culture. The second is that the Western church has at the same time increasingly allowed itself to be contaminated, infiltrated and compromised by its host culture.

The first point is no surprise. Throughout history, the church of Christ has always faced forces that sought to deflect it from its mission. Even when the church played a dominant role in the West, becoming the official religion throughout Europe and, unofficially, the dominant religion in the United States as well, it constantly faced political and other compromises to its integrity and authenticity. Quite how Christians and the church should relate to the culture in which they find themselves has, of course, been the subject of much argument and debate throughout Christendom's history.

But regardless of how Christians ought to relate to their culture, most of us would agree that the West's post-Christian, secularized cultural climate is increasingly unwelcoming of, or even actively hostile to, the gospel of Jesus Christ. Assuming that is correct, however, doesn't give Christians any excuses for where they find themselves today. This book's second point, that the contemporary Western church has allowed itself to be unduly contaminated by its host culture, is no surprise either. Here too, the church has throughout its history needed to resist the seductions of every culture it has encountered—sometimes with greater success, sometimes with less. This book flows from the conviction that the contemporary Western church, whether in Europe or North America, is in serious danger of succumbing to the lures, temptations and pressures of its host culture, so much so that it is in danger of forsaking aspects of its Christ-given mandate of being his agent where he has placed it.

Far from interacting with our cultural milieu thoughtfully and selectively, we have either been uncertain on how or what to resist, or easily succumbed to inviting seemingly innocent but ultimately unbiblical values into our lives and our churches, values like materialism, individualism and an obsession with celebrities and entertainment.

This book is intended to remind all of us who are committed to seeing the church live out its mission without compromise or contamination that we have our work cut out for us. Hence this collection of brief satires, which are directed mainly at the church in the United States. (The church in Europe operates in a far more secularized setting than in the United States, although in this country too Christians frequently find themselves a minority voice in their schools, their workplaces, and their communities.)

Some of the entries speak to the unwelcome reception Jesus and the gospel message would receive in the contemporary United States. Others poke fun at ways in which the church has bought into a troublingly Western way of doing things. But all are designed to help Christians ask the questions, "Do my own

Christian faith and my local church need to shake off some of the dust of our culture?" and, "Are we as alert as we should be to those aspects of our culture that run counter to the character of what Christ would have us be?"

Hosea chapter 13, like so many other places in the Old Testament, speaks of God rescuing the children of Israel from the desert, only to see them forsake him and his love after they reach the Promised Land. The problem, or at least part of it, was the special set of seductions that came with the new territory: the lure of false gods, a temptation to set up a king so they could be just like everyone else, and the always present temptation to forget whence they had come and how they had been rescued. Maybe they would have been much better off spiritually if, instead of settling whole-heartedly into the promised land and as comfortably as they did, they had lived at the desert's edge—with one foot in the territory that reminded them constantly of their legacy and God's grace in the past, and the other foot in the promised land, to remind them to remain a set-apart people in the present.

We too should think about the dangers of living with both feet in secular, often hostile but always beguiling territory. Rather, keeping one foot in the desert, as we straddle the border, should help us be more mindful of our legacy and how we are to function in territory that is not our ultimate home. Malcolm Muggeridge had it right when he said of Christians, "The only ultimate disaster that can befall us is to feel ourselves at home on this earth."

Changes in the environment the church faces may be so subtle day by day, month by month, that it's only when we step back and look at a span of 20 years, for example, that we see just how much has changed. The kind of explicit sexual content now routinely and abundantly available on U.S. TV was not tolerated in TV's early decades. Changes in the moral climate typically happen slowly, over decades rather than overnight. In rare in-stances, such as Supreme Court decisions on abortion laws, we can point to a particular "before and after" shift in the culture. But mostly we don't wake up one morning and say, "Hey, who shifted these cultural expectations during the night?" The climate changes slowly and subtly.

Given this reality, it is important now and again for the church to take stock by asking, "What *is* the environment in which we're operating? And to what extent *are* we accommodating ourselves to that environment?" This book is not suggesting for a moment that the church should disengage from the world, and that Christians should flee from a hostile culture to our own enclaves, where we can huddle together for warmth against the secular chill. On the contrary, God appoints us to serve as "the salt of the earth" and "the light of the world." (Matt 5:13–14) Ours is a mandate to engage the world, not withdraw from it. How we do that is a task for every generation of Christians to learn anew, in whatever place we find ourselves. This book does not presume to prescribe for you or your church some formula for attaining that delicate balance. Rather, it is intended to serve as an alarm-clock ring for those Christians and local churches that may need a wake-up call because (to mix metaphors) they or their churches have strayed too far into hostile territory, or feel far more comfortable living there than they should. To that end, some of the pieces here may seem provocative, even offensive. That's not their intent. Rather, the objective is to seek fresh ways to honor Paul's admonition in Romans 12:2: "Do not conform any longer to the pattern of this world, but be transformed by the renewing of your mind."

Benjamin Franklin once commented: "Strange, that a man who has wit enough to write a satire should have folly enough to publish it." This book is an invitation for you to benefit from that act of folly. My hope is therefore that the God who used a donkey to speak to an unwilling Balaam will in some modest way use even the realm of satire to accomplish His purposes in our lives and His Kingdom.

The Truly Personalized
Family Worship Experience

Hello, I'm Sandy, and I'll be your worship leader today. Is this your first visit to St. John's?

Well then, an especially warm welcome to you. We've just introduced a whole new order of service—here, let me give each of you a bulletin. Also, let me tell you about our special today. The pastor's special is a brief homily on grace, which you can have with either Arminian or Calvinist flavoring. And that comes of course with your choice of one hymn or two praise songs, plus an intercessory prayer for any person or need of your choosing.

Meanwhile, would you like to start with a little praise music? No? OK, I'll give you a few minutes to look over the bulletin and I'll be right back. And here's the children's bulletin for you, young lady, and some crayons.

[And, a few minutes later. . . .]

Are you ready to order? Good. What will you have, then, ma'am? The special? And you want hymn no. 203. Is that with the choir or without? And you still want to think about the prayer; no problem.

And what about you, young lady? You want the number three children's story, about Sammy the Saintly Squirrel. Great. We've never had a kid yet who didn't just love Sammy. He's one of my favorites too!

And you sir, have you decided? Number 7, the beatitudes sampler. Excellent choice. With a side of silent meditation? Of course. Would you like the two minute or the four minute? The four minute? I see we're really spiritually hungry tonight! And hold all the music? Can do.

Anything else I can get you?

No? Great. As I said, my name is Sandy, and if there's anything I can do . . . .

What's that, sir?

I understand, lots of people ask. No, the service charge isn't included.

2

A Recently Discovered Fragment
from Luke Chapter 11

"One day, Jesus was praying in a certain place. When he finished, one of his disciples said to him, 'Lord, teach us to pray, just as John taught his disciples.'"

—LUKE 11:1

Jesus answered, "When you pray, say: 'Lord, we just want to thank you, Lord, for, like, bringing us together today, Lord, and for just being who you are, Lord, and Lord, for just blessing us so much, Lord, that we like don't know how to thank you, Lord, for, like, all you've done for us, Lord, but we just praise your great and holy name, Lord and we just thank you so much, Lord, for. . . .'"

And the disciples said, "But we already pray like that, Lord. Any other suggestions?"

Jesus said, "OK, how about this: When you pray, say: Our Father. . . ."

3

Donald Trump Deals with the Trinity

"What we have is a nation where everyone is his own favorite theologian."

—George Barna

Donald Trump is close to resolving a longstanding personal theological crisis and may decide as early as tomorrow to fire one of the three members of the Trinity, said sources close to the business magnate.

The move follows growing pressure Trump has felt to downsize his theological commitments, said one of his aides, speaking anonymously because he was not authorized to comment on what he described as "an extremely difficult spiritual choice."

Trump has long been known to be uncomfortable with what he has privately described as the "inherent inefficiencies of the God-in-three-persons" model.

Another aide, also speaking anonymously, said, "It's possible that instead of actually cutting back the size of the Trinity he may rely on much more outsourcing of the work they do."

Archibald Dutton, a professor of theology at Yale Divinity School, said it would be difficult to predict how Trump might decide. "Mr. Trump could of course decide to fire any one of the three members of the Trinity. If he believes strongly in the 'three-in-one' and 'one-in-three' doctrine, he may be satisfied that there is a high level of cross training among them and that any two of them could pick up the slack."

Many analysts have speculated that if Trump were to give a pink slip to any members of the Trinity, God the Father would be the most likely choice as the cost savings would be enormous. Trump, who is known for his bold moves, may decide to fire God the Father simply to show who is in charge of his theology.

But Dutton thought such a choice unlikely, "for symbolic and political reasons." He added, "Firing Jesus would also present great difficulties, but of a different kind: he is highly popular with certain market segments. However, he can be a very divisive figure, who often comes across to those outside the church as intolerant and narrow."

And what of the Holy Spirit? Fr. Albert McGilkey, a theologian at Notre Dame University, said if Trump were to fire anyone, the least controversial choice would certainly be the Holy Spirit. "He's the least prominent member of the Trinity and many people, to be honest, have only the murkiest idea of what his actual job description is." McGilkey added, "In reality, many people have already dismissed the Holy Spirit from their personal theologies, so a decision by Mr. Trump to do the same is likely to be far less controversial."

Another option, but according to most sources highly unlikely, is for Trump to fire the entire Trinity and go completely godless. But some observers have not ruled out that possibility. According to Candace Helmbach, a professor of cultural studies at the University of Toledo, "When it comes to their theology, most Americans don't get this Trinity idea anyway, according to the polls we've seen." She added, "Most of them would probably support Trump whatever he does, whether it involves breaking up what many Americans increasingly see as an ineffective three-person team, or merely replacing them with another set of convictions altogether."

4

Go Into All the World . . . An Invitation to Missions

"In the Middle Ages, people were tourists because of their religion, whereas now they are tourists because tourism is their religion."

—ROBERT RUNCIE,
FORMER ARCHBISHOP OF CANTERBURY

Join us this Christmas break, when Pastor Schrick will once again lead a group as part of our "Mexico Mission" initiative to the desperately poor village of Xitoplaca en los Baños, just 12 miles outside the fabulous resort location of Luxurio de la Playa.

In keeping with Pastor Schrick's philosophy that the typical week-long or 10-day mission trips are rushed and not especially meaningful, we will spend a full two weeks in Mexico.

THE PROVISIONAL ITINERARY:

Day 1:

Travel day

Days 2–4:

We stay at the resort town of Luxurio de la Playa, for three days of briefing and learning about the social, economic and spiritual dynamics of those to whom we minister. The resort hotel is wonderfully quiet and alive (with great nightlife!) at the same time. We'll have plenty of time for the three R's: Rest, Recreation and Reflection on what we are learning, and to allow for easy cultural adjustment. And don't worry, ladies, there'll be ample time for shopping at local markets!

Days 5–7:

We'll then spend three days in an air-conditioned coach, with a professional driver and guide. During this time we'll see at first hand more of the rich heritage of the Xitoplaca region. Highlights will include the astonishing Guadeleco Ruins and the spectacular Fuentes Waterfall. We'll stay in at least 3- and 4-star accommodations along the way.

Day 8:

A high point of the trip for many is the morning we put all our preparation to work and actually visit Xitoplaca en los Baños. We will meet Pastor Sanchez of the village church, for whom we will help fund another much needed addition to his house. This will be the fifth room we've added to what is widely admired in the village as a typical American home. Pastor Sanchez tells us his home serves as a real inspiration to many of the villagers, as they see the gospel's practical applications to their hopes of escaping the desperate grip of poverty.

We "get our hands dirty" and practice our Spanish as we chat with the local laborers. Mid-morning the ladies of the village will serve us local delicacies and the children will sing and dance for us. That afternoon, it's on to the adjoining village, Xitoplaco de los Mas Pobres, with which we have been working on developing another partner church relationship. If time permits, and temperatures aren't in the high 80s or 90s, we'll get off the bus for a few minutes to build our relationship with the villagers.

Tip: Remember to bring your cameras (you won't *believe* how cute these kids are!), plenty of bottled water, sunscreen and hand sanitizer.

Finally, in the evening, Pastor Sanchez will host a cheese and wine reception for us to thank us for our ministry and support. (The reception will be at our hotel; some people in our groups have found coping with the dust and heat in the village to be a challenge.)

Days 9–11:

We conclude our mission trip with a three days' debrief at a serene resort in Cancun (at least 4-stars).

Days 12–13:

Then you're on your own for the last three days. You can either continue your stay at the Cancun resort and rest, or if you're more adventurous arrange a side trip through the hotel's travel desk.

Day 14:

Travel day

Cost is $3,500 (double occupancy)
Contact Bea in the church office for sign-up information.

5

What a Friend We Have in Jesus

To the tune of "What a Friend We Have in Jesus"

What a friend I have in Jesus, I had sought him everywhere.
Now on Facebook I have found him, seven million friends we
    share.
If you're feeling lost and lonely, social networks are the key,
Go online and message Jesus, and be friends with him and me.

He's a friend who's always faithful, he's unfailingly on call,
Any time you want to tag him or just write upon his wall.
For he is your online savior, and no matter how you feel,
Know he'll also be beside you if you get a life that's real.

6

Carol's Busy Day

- Get wedding present for Tim at Macy's (try for that $300 espresso machine)

- Visit the Nordstrom's half-year sale

- Mail in the $1,000-a-plate dinner reservations for the Senator's re-election campaign

- Take Jonathan to polo practice

- Make airline reservation for Abby's college visits to Bryn Mawr, Dartmouth and Princeton

- Confirm appointment with Abby's college-selection counselor

- Call the interior decorator about the designer staircase for house remodel

- Take the BMW in for a service

- Mail in $25 contribution for Sisters of Mercy Inner City poverty relief

7

The Jesus Christ Show: The Credits

. . . . Thank you Jesus!

And so we come to the end of another "Word of the Lord," hosted by none other than Jesus Christ himself.

Please join us again next week, when we'll be back with another life-changing hour of ministry with our Lord. Next week, he'll tell us about the real people on whom he based the story of the Prodigal Son. Then, his special guests will be Larry King and former President Jimmy Carter. Finally, he'll debate with a couple of non-believing physics professors from a major research university on the nature of miracles. He promises we can expect a big surprise or two, and so can they, he says!

Many thanks to the wonderful people of Santa Barbara, where we were broadcasting live today. Next week we'll be coming to you from Safeco Field in the wonderful city of Seattle.

Thanks too to Dollar Car Rental for transportation.

Accommodation was provided by Westin Hotels.

Financial services were provided by Bank of America.

Our Lord's wardrobe was provided by Holy Dudes Outfitters, of San Diego.

Hairstyling was by Henri's of Hollywood.

"Word of the Lord" is brought to you by Messiah Enterprises, Inc., a Time-Warner company.

Thank you, good night, and may the Lord bless you and keep you and make his face to shine upon you!

(Applause)

8

The "Good WUC" Man

"So he made a whip out of cords,
and drove all from the temple area . . ."

—JOHN 2:15

When Danielle Plummer's fiancé popped the question to her in Chicago early in June, it took only a few moments after she'd said "yes" before her thoughts turned to another man altogether: Eddie McKenzie. While her fiancé is the reason for the wedding, McKenzie is the man who'll make it affordable.

McKenzie, a 38-year-old former youth pastor from Indiana, has single handedly created a new role in the increasingly high cost enterprise of the contemporary church wedding: the wedding underwriting coordinator, or "WUC." McKenzie cheerfully and repeatedly refers to himself as the "Good WUC man every girl needs if she's to get the wedding of her dreams," he says. "Guys typically don't give a rip about the frills and the flowers—they just want it over." But with the average church wedding now costing more than $27,000, even the most generous bride's parents are unable and increasingly unwilling to help out.

And that's where McKenzie works his magic, by brokering deals between churches and local merchants and national companies whose advertising can cut the cost of a typical wedding by as much as 30 percent. McKenzie explains: "When I get a church to buy into a sponsorship package, it becomes a win-win situation for everyone. The church will carry ads—on printed media like their bulletins and church newsletters, on their websites, on notice boards and reader boards outside, and with discrete announcements during worship as well." He explains that the worship service announcements typically meet some resistance, "but they're fairly discreet, more like Public TV underwriting than your regular hard sell ad."

All this helps the bride-to-be, because the churches' contracts with the advertisers guarantee that most of that revenue will be passed on to help the young couple. This help comes not only in the expected ways of reducing the traditional fees pastors receive for weddings, or the rental of the church facilities and even the catering for a reception that may happen in the church hall afterwards. It goes further than that, because in the typical wedding at a larger church a bride and groom will get up to $1,500 to put toward whatever else they want: the bride's dress, the honeymoon, or anything else.

Each church sets its own guidelines on who's eligible for these wedding rebates, typically limiting them to couples who've been members for at least a year or two. "But that's entirely up to the church, on how they want to handle that," says McKenzie. The trick to making this work, he emphasizes, is the flexibility the local church has in spending its ad revenue.

Of course, national and even local advertisers are looking for returns on their spending, which means that McKenzie targets churches with weekly attendances of at least 1,000. Bigger is obviously better. He explains that the contracts between the advertisers and the churches are complex, to ensure the companies get the exposure they're paying for. "By and large, though, the larger churches have mostly steady attendance and because the churches provide audited headcounts of services, the system generally works largely as everyone expects."

The scheme isn't without its critics. McKenzie readily admits that some churches resist what they call "commercial creep into the sanctuary," as one Methodist bishop put it. But McKenzie isn't worried about these objections. "Typically, they're coming from smaller churches which, quite frankly, I suspect are tasting sour grapes because they don't have the drawing power to interest advertisers in the first place."

In Danielle Plummer's case, she's been a member at First Celebration Church in the Chicago suburb of Glen Ellyn for seven years, and says she expects to get all wedding costs waived by the church. In addition, she and her fiancé, Jay Butzke, will get a check for just on $1,200 to do with what they like. "We'll put this toward the reception," she said, which they're holding at a nearby restaurant.

The impact of the Good WUC Man on Danielle's and Jay's service will be typical for their church, Danielle said. In addition to inserts in the wedding bulletin for a local pizza merchant, two dry cleaners and a windshield repair company, the bulletin itself will carry ads for Holiday Inn (one of the first and largest national sponsors to have worked with McKenzie), Bride magazine, and Northwest Mutual Life insurance company. In addition, McKenzie says Danielle's and Jay's wedding will also include "three or four discreet product announcements in the service itself, all OK'd by the officiating pastor."

What's next? McKenzie's novel approach is not only being copied, with varying degrees of success, in other cities. But he too is opening branch offices in Los Angeles, Dallas and Boston, with other major cities lined up as possibilities. Nor is he limiting himself to weddings, he says. "There's no reason why this couldn't also work for funerals," he adds. "It didn't take us long to overcome the fears that somehow commercials were detracting from a wedding; on the contrary, we proved they could enhance the couple's special day. But while funerals will be a tougher sell, I think many churches are more ready for this option than you might think." He added: "It may take a while, but people will inevitably accept this is simply a step toward wiser stewardship."

9

Case 1495/94: Simon Peter

Patient is a 37-year-old male, and a professional fisherman. He was brought to Holy Mother of Mercy clinic on April 30 by city police. He had been placed in preventive custody after displaying psychotic behaviors and defying authorities' instructions not to disturb the peace with stories about a religious leader who had returned to life.

Patient has an engaging, enthusiastic manner, and is surprisingly articulate for someone with no college education. He manifested numerous delusional tendencies, besides his conviction that the religious cult leader, the so-called "Jesus of Nazareth" who was executed last month, has now come back to life. The patient's conviction that this has happened is unswerving. He presents himself as mostly rational, conceding that people just don't rise from the dead. He insisted, however, that the cult leader had "promised" he would do so and that patient had seen him on several occasions since the execution, talking with him and on one occasion even having a meal with the man.

But patient's apparently rational disposition was contradicted by three other self-reported incidents. On one occasion, he said that he was out in his fishing boat when Jesus came walking to him on the water. Patient said the cult leader invited him to do likewise, and that he was able to take several steps himself before beginning to sink. He insisted that he would have been able to keep walking if it were not for his "lack of faith."

A second instance involved him going on a hiking trip with the leader and a few other cult followers. At some point the leader "turned a brilliant white," and was joined by two long dead prophets of the cult. After some time of conversation between the leader and the prophets, the two prophets "vanished into a cloud."

The third and most recent instance occurred last week after being arrested for disturbing the peace, when he escaped in what is now widely known as the "Touched by an Angel" jail break. Patient still insists, as he did in earlier media interviews, that an "angel" led him out of the county jail.

Patient does not seem overtly self-destructive but referred several times to a possible "martyr's death" that the leader had prophesied for him. A suicide watch is therefore recommended.

I also would recommend starting Thorazine 25 mg twice a day and continue involuntary stay at Holy Mother of Mercy psychiatric unit for patient's self-protection. As an added precaution, place double security guard at door. Finally, I would recommend trying to contact the family and his rabbi.

Signed:
Connie McAfee, MD, Admitting physician
Copy to hospital security

10

The Healer

Once upon a time there was prophet in a far away land who had remarkable gifts of healing. People brought all their illnesses and infirmities before him, and out of his love for everyone he healed them all. He turned no one away. They would bring him their cancers and their heart problems, their failing livers and their emphysema.

They began to bring him other problems too, like the young man who brought his low self-esteem, but could not afford counseling. So the prophet healed him right away. Then there was the young woman who came to him and said, "I want to develop a more authentic self." And she too did he heal. Once there was a man who brought his laptop computer, which was sorely troubled and could not be hooked up to his home network. The man told the prophet that he had spent many, many hours on the phone trying to get tech support, but without success. The prophet placed his hand on the laptop and said, "Go, try it now. Your faith has made it whole."

A rich man came to him one day, asking the prophet to heal his battered and bruised investment portfolio. "It took a terrible beating when the housing and financial markets collapsed," he said. "While I once had much, now I have little," he said. And the people who were in the crowd asked the prophet, "Was it this man's greed or that of his parents that caused his portfolio to suffer?"

The prophet did not answer, for his heart was heavy. He walked away, shaking the dust off his feet. As he did so, several in the crowd called after him, "And could you do something about these dirt roads?"

11

The Trial

*"If you were arrested for being a Christian, would
there be enough evidence to convict you?"*

—DAVID OTIS FULLER

It wasn't the verdict itself that was the surprise, as much as how
lopsided the jury was in its decision: a unanimous 12–0, finding
all twenty-six defendants innocent of the charge that they were
Christians.

The verdict followed an unusual experiment conducted by
Calvary Center, a 3,300 member non-denominational church in
San Diego, and the law school at nearby Arbor Crest University,
a Christian school.

The idea began when Calvary Center's senior pastor, Jim
Trovato, and the dean of the law school, Chuck Zerkin, were
speaking during one of their regular racquetball games.

"I remember asking Chuck if our church members lived
lives that truly set them apart from their non-Christian neighbors and colleagues," said Trovato. "What if they were accused of
being Christians—do you think they'd be found guilty?

"Well, we played around with this idea and the next thing
we had a moot court set up, where some of the Christian law
students put on trial thirty of our members who'd agreed to take
part in this. For various reasons, four had to pull out, so we were
left with twenty-six of them."

Zerkin said that one team of students researched the lives of the church members, acting as prosecutors and trying to find as much evidence as they could to convince a student jury that the Christians were "guilty as charged." Another team of students acted as a defense team.

"What was disturbing," said Zerkin, "was how easily and quickly the defense shot down the prosecution's case. The defense showed that the twenty-six Christians were in virtually every respect just like their secular neighbors and other people with whom they interacted."

Emmy Perle, a final-year law student on the defense team, said her task was amazingly easy. "I mean, there was nothing that set the Christians apart from others. Their lifestyles were largely the same, they lived in the same kinds of houses as their neighbors, they earned the same kinds of salaries, and they spent it on the same kinds of things. For example, they drove the same proportion of SUVs as the rest of the community, and took the same kind of spendy holidays in Europe and the Caribbean as everyone else."

Perle said her defense team was worried that when they looked closely at deeper values, they would find more radical differences that would set the Christians apart. "But even here," she said, "we found that their charitable giving was only slightly higher than others in the community. Many of them had been divorced, despite the high premium their faith supposedly puts on marriage. And most had lived together before they got married." In addition, Perle added, "Many of the younger Christians do at least some recreational drugs."

Johnny Binder, another final-year law student who led the prosecution team, lamented that "all of us students, on both the defense and the prosecution, thought this would be a fun exercise, but we were pretty sobered by how hard it was to find anything truly positive to pin on these good people that set them apart." Binder added: "About the only thing we could point to was their involvement in church activities, but the defense destroyed that argument with evidence that non-Christians are just as much engaged in their own clubs and volunteer activities."

Ketitia Allan, another student on the defense team, said: "It made us all think just how we're probably no different from these other Christians. Many of us go to Calvary Center, and we'd assumed these people were great Christian role models for us.

"I suppose we still do, but somehow I need to look at things differently now as I think about my own faith and my calling as a lawyer," said Allan, who plans to pursue a career in celebrity law.

12

The Demographic Report

Jim:

I'm e-mailing you the highlights from the latest demographics, which I'm afraid look bleak indeed. On almost every front things look bad for Jesus. The support that looked so good on Palm Sunday has essentially evaporated, and it's plain that Jesus will need to do something dramatic soon if he's to avoid being totally rejected by public opinion.

Here are some specifics for you to share with the campaign team. I've attached an Excel document with the fuller figures, and you'll get the full printout via FedEx tomorrow.

In every key demographic group he's now registering less than 10 percent approvals. Income, education, ethnic group, occupation, and even religious affiliation show no significant differences. In fact, the more devout Jews seem even more hostile than ever, registering only 4 percent. (And even with our standard margin of error in the poll of 3.5 percent either way, he'd still be at a negligible 7.5 percent even in the most optimistic of interpretations.)

Curiously, two groups do show slightly better numbers. One is the odd assortment of individuals who fall into a psychographic group we've labeled "social peripherals"—the hookers, tax collectors, unemployed, chronically poor, and so on. But even though this group gives Jesus an inexplicably high 47 percent approval, they're essentially worthless to his campaign because of their traditionally appallingly low voter turnout. Their potential to influence his campaign is virtually non-existent.

The other group are those self-identifying as Samaritans, who give him a 23 percent approval. Quite why this would be so high calls for more analysis, and normally we'd be looking at setting up some focus groups to check into this. But we can't spare the time, given how desperate the overall picture is.

To be blunt, Jim, I'm afraid we're at the point where the campaign team probably has to tell Jesus to look at withdrawing from the race. A carefully worded statement saying he had never sought political office in the first place, that others have misread his intentions, and so on, could allow him to leave with his head held high. The record clearly indicates that he's never explicitly said he was a candidate, as you know. Yes, the media will accuse him of being deceptive, but I'm sure he can easily weather that.

For now, though, we need to think about putting together a news conference announcing his withdrawal. I'm confident that when he sees the numbers and after he's listened to the rest of you, he'll see that we really have no choice.

Assuming he agrees, I'll tell Hal in the morning to line up a location for the announcement. I'm thinking of the Hotel Gethsemane.

13

From the Bench

Will the accused please stand. I would not normally go to the trouble of addressing the court in what might otherwise be seen as a routine instance of a breach of the peace. But given the publicity your conduct has generated, I feel compelled to speak up.

I don't think you have any idea how much you have offended this community by your behavior at the cathedral last week. When you chased out members of the staff who were changing money and providing the necessary animals for worshipers' sacrifices, you not only brought utter chaos to a holy place but you terrorized these innocent men and women who were merely going about their business. Various cathedral employees have testified how upsetting this whole incident was, and you yourself saw the cashier in the cathedral gift shop break down on the witness stand when she described how traumatized she was by the panicked goats rushing through the store.

Now, I'm not terribly excited about small animal sacrifices myself, and I don't know if yours was an animal rights concern. You certainly haven't helped your case today by refusing to say anything in your defense. As you heard, two of the arresting officers said you claimed this was "your father's house" during the incident. Whatever your personal religious views, and I try not to get into theological questions in this court room, you cannot conduct yourself this way. I don't know if this is how you would normally do things this way out in the boondocks where you're from, but don't even think about repeating this kind of behavior in this city again.

Because this is your first offence, and because you can thank God nobody got hurt in the stampede you caused, I'm putting you on two years probation. I am requiring you, however, to attend a court-approved anger management course. Your probation officer will work out those details with you. You seem to be a sincere and devout man, and maybe with some counseling you can avoid this kind of foolishness in the future.

And to the members of the media, let me say that I will not be granting any interviews.

Court is adjourned.

14

Palestine Politics—The Week in Review

(Transcript no. 3894)

. . . . and getting that supplemental spending bill was a compromise that left neither Herod nor Pilate happy, Bill.

Bill: Right. Well, let's look now at what that mystery man, Jesus of Nazareth has been up to this week.

Tim: Yes, once again one curious development after another. Clearly, you have here a man whom both the Democrats and the Republicans would dearly love to run on their ticket. All the polls are showing he could sweep away whichever side he ran against, and his following has just kept growing. He's got such charisma that he could get on the phone and virtually call in his order to either party and tell them what he wants, and he'd get it.

Bill: Exactly, but if that's what he's planning to do, and keep us all in suspense to drum up even more interest, he's certainly not winning friends as he goes about this.

Tim: The man in fact seems to be going out of his way to insult and taunt the leadership in both parties. He's really thrown the book at them, called them hypocrites and painted tombs—not the sort of thing you want to say to people with whom you're going to work in government, or even if you're going to have to deal with them as an opposition.

Bill: Well, the man's new to politics, Tim, and he's admittedly surrounded himself with the most unorthodox bunch of advisors, none of whom have any political background.

Tim: Except for that fellow, Simon the Zealot.

Bill: True, but then that's offset by that arch representative of the establishment, Matthew the tax guy.

Tim: Still, the point is, doesn't this man realize the stakes he's playing for? I have to believe he's smarter than this, but it almost looks as if he's this country bumpkin, coming to town with this bunch of hick supporters, playing the role of the populist as he takes jabs at the party leaders.

Bill: And neither party is going to take kindly to that. Then what do you make of that extraordinary business in the Temple this week, where he drove out everyone on this pretense of moral or religious purity?

Tim: Again, at exactly the time he should be creating alliances, he's doing exactly the opposite. And it's not as if he seems to have some kind of anger management issue; everyone who saw this said it was a very controlled, deliberate kind of thing. Then there's that bizarre turn of events with the TV ads. Everyone thought his campaign would just shrivel and die when he turned his back on running any kind of ads, but in spite of that he has the most astonishingly successful name recognition a candidate could hope for.

Bill: Right. Either that's an incredibly brilliant masterstroke, or else plain good luck. All the pundits are putting it down to luck; the man clearly has so much going for him, but he obviously doesn't have a clue on how to run for office. And yet, never have we seen a race like this where a complete novice could come out on top. Well, we're running out of time. Check in next week with us here at Palestine Politics in Review. Who knows what this totally unpredictable Jesus of Nazareth will have done by then. Good night.

Tim: Goodnight.

15

The Bracelet

Needing to choose between I-205, which was a longer drive but probably had less traffic, and I-5, straight into the city, Jesus glanced for the fourteenth time that morning at his "What Would I Do?" bracelet.

16

Minutes of the Church Governing Council

June 18—An Excerpt

. . . $8,900 for the new digital reader board.

Worship services: Following lengthy discussion the church council agreed to the new series of worship services proposed by Pastor Brady, following the report received last month from Abundant Life Consulting services. Based on ALC's demographic and psychographic analysis of those worshipping at our church, Pastor Brady said we should devise four ministry streams to cater to four adult worship client groups. ALC identified these groups as Young Seekers, Disrupted Mid-Lifers, Disaffected Professionals, and Mature Walkers.

While these different groups have some overlap, their general life styles and interests tend to be quite different, Pastor Brady explained. As a result, the Young Seekers service will be offered on Saturday night, with contemporary music and a highly informal atmosphere. The service will be held in Fellowship Hall, to avoid the uncomfortable feel of the sanctuary for this group. That location will also allow for easy installation of the sushi bar that ALC recommended.

The Disrupted Mid-Lifers, mostly in their 30s and 40s, are marked by people in transition: divorce, newcomers to town, those who are currently unemployed, or who are otherwise dealing with major personal issues. This segment won't in fact have a conventional service at all, said Pastor Brady, but will instead meet in a series of support groups provided during the week.

Most will be held on Wednesday nights, when childcare will be available at the church.

The Disaffected Professionals need to be treated with special care, the ALC report stated. Potentially the largest group of giving units to the church, both in numbers and in total amount, this group has great difficulty with many of the church's traditional theological positions, either rejecting some teachings outright or quietly disregarding others. More concerned with issues of social justice, self-improvement and personal health, the Disaffected Professionals barely tolerate even the kind of contemporary service planned for the Young Seekers. Accordingly, we will offer a 9 a.m. non-traditional service focusing on personal growth issues, which de-emphasizes traditional worship components. This group is hungry for personal spiritual development, according to the ALC report. Supplementing this non-doctrinal, more inclusive worship approach will be a series of community volunteer opportunities (no longer to be called "mission" or "ministry," both of which have negative connotations for this group) in the community.

Those comprising the Mature Walkers segment, by far the smallest, are typically in their mid-50s and older. Strong traditionalists and the most resistant to change, this group feels most comfortable meeting in the sanctuary at 11 a.m. on Sundays. This service represents a continuation of our present programming. The ALC study indicated, however, that numbers for this group continue to dwindle, and it was recommended that the Church Council conduct an ongoing cost-benefit analysis to see at what point the traditionally larger financial support from this group is exceeded by the maintenance costs of the sanctuary and other ancillary costs like that of the probable need for major organ repairs in the next few years. It was Moved/Seconded/Approved that Pastor Brady chair a task force to begin looking at possible alternate uses in future for the sanctuary space.

Report from the Church Unity Task Force: Betty Bonser reported on the progress . . . .

Petrusco vs. Lake City Tabernacle

Washington. AP. The Supreme Court will begin hearing arguments tomorrow in a case that could radically curtail religious expression, especially for those faiths committed to winning converts to their ranks.

The case, Petrusco vs. Lake City Tabernacle, arises from a Los Angeles man who successfully sued a small church in Florida when he was offended by a sermon he heard when visiting the church. Jimmy Petrusco, who describes himself as an agnostic, attended worship with his parents when the pastor preached on the need for repentance from one's sins. Petrusco successfully argued in state courts that he had suffered emotional distress at having to listen to what he described as intolerant teaching. A Federal Appeals court overturned the decision, on First Amendment grounds, but the Supreme Court agreed last fall to take the case because, the Court said, it raises substantial questions about the newly emerging legal doctrines of "toleration advocacy" and "offensiveness minimization." With conflicting rulings on these issues coming from three Federal districts, the Supreme Court essentially had no choice but to take on the issue.

For churches and other religious groups that hold firm doctrines that have exclusivist aspects, the stakes are enormous. The cases in the lower courts have reflected a battle between freedom of expression and freedom of religion rights on the one hand, in accordance with long established legal precedents. On the other side are two sets of bold but as yet unestablished legal claims.

One is that people have a right to protection from offensive viewpoints. Drawing on obscenity law, and the right not to have to be exposed to unwelcome material, advocates of this position argue that free expression rights are secondary to the right not to be offended. The second set of arguments is that public interest demands that the courts protect tolerance as a virtue, again at the expense of free expression when necessary.

These arguments, if successful, would gut all religious activities that make outsiders uncomfortable with their message, and would prohibit religious groups from critiquing other faiths. Thus, as a Federal case in New Jersey revealed, it would be illegal for a Christian church to teach that those of other beliefs are "lost" unless they become Christians.

Analysts are unclear how the Supreme Court might rule in this case. It has received an unprecedented number of "friend of the court" briefs, especially on behalf of religious groups, but from those arguing for the other side too. Most church leaders and numerous representatives of other religious groups have raised grave concerns about the implications of a ruling against their position. "This case threatens the very heart of the Christian message," said Catholic Bishop Antonio Escobar.

But other clergy have argued that all the ruling would do is to require Christianity and other religions to be more open and tolerant. "Who on earth can oppose more welcoming religions?" asked the Rev. Annabelle Amistad, a pastor at a non-denominational church in New York. She added, "Churches and other places of worship are supposed to be welcoming, accepting and tolerant. And it's only the closed-minded churches that are opposing the tolerance movement. If this goes the way I hope it does, these intolerant types will be forced to change."

The Court is expected to announce its ruling by late spring.

18

An E-mail on Choosing the Disciples

Dear Sir:

We at Solid Rock Executive Searches are pleased to report our progress on recruiting your leadership team of disciples. While we respect your desire to limit the size of your team to 12, we believe this may be unduly restrictive as you seek to implement your ministry objectives. Nevertheless, for now we have identified the dozen slots we think you most need to fill, and we remain available for consultation should you wish to expand the size of the group.

Rather than identifying and recruiting individual disciples, the course you had requested, we have taken the liberty of employing the more conventional approach of identifying the job functions first. After receiving your approval for the composition of the team, as we have outlined it below, we will gladly move into the recruitment phase.

Here are the dozen positions we believe you need most as you prepare to launch your ministry. These are not ranked in order of priority. All positions are full time.

1. Church relations specialist
2. Finance manager
3. Fund raiser
4. Government relations specialist
5. Legal counsel

6. Logistics and planning specialist

7. Marketing manager

8. Media relations specialist

9. Personal assistant

10. Pollster

11. Speech writer

12. Web designer

If budgeting permits, we urge you to consider including on the team—even if in a part-time capacity—one or more of the following: risk management specialist; wardrobe manager; hair stylist; music consultant; personal trainer; and security officer.

We wish to assure you as we move ahead on this project that we will do our utmost to provide you a team that has both gender and ethnic balance. Please let us know as soon as possible your response to our suggestions.

Sincerely,
Eric Lamberton
Senior consultant

19

The Update—A Phone Call

*"Go into all the world and preach the good news
to all creation."*

—MARK 16:15

OK, so let me give you what I've got. Yeah, on Paul. No surprise there—that was a long shot anyway; he's booked out three years in advance, minimum.

I've put out some feelers with a few of the apostles—Peter, James, John, you know, the biggies. Also, I've tried getting Apollos but I haven't been able to reach his agent yet. Yeah, I know he's not as big a name as the others but he really is an incredible speaker. I think he'd be perfect for the conference. But I'll keep trying for the others.

What? Costs? We're looking at a minimum of ten grand for the weekend, for any of these guys. Paul gets that much just for one day, depending on the group. Anyway, I know Peter's still a possibility. His agent's checking some dates and other possible commitments—some media appearances and a Holy Land tour he might be leading. But he's also pretty steep—not so much his speaker's fee, but with all the extras. He always takes his wife wherever he goes, sometimes his mother-in-law, and we'd have to pick up the tab on that. They only fly first class, and go for the five star hotel routine, and all that. So before you know it, you're much in the same bracket as Paul.

Yes, I agree; Peter would be perfect but I don't know if the committee will go for that kind of expense. But we first need to see if he's available. Who? John? Yes, that could work—again depending on dates. But that guy's a pain in the butt with all his books and stuff. We have to pay to ship all the stuff here, from his organization, ship back what's left over, and staff the book table all the time he's with us. His people won't sign a contract without all that. We'll need to tie up at least three of the conference people to push all those autographed gospels, DVDs, videos and so on. I heard that at a typical conference he can easily net five grand just from sales. But I guess that's what the people want.

Well, we're still two years out but I think we've got to line up someone this month if we want to have a shot at one of the big names in ministry. Look, I'll keep you posted. I'm hoping to hear back from a couple of these guys in the next day or two. I'm pretty sure we can have something locked in place by the weekend.

OK. Yeah, I'll tell him. And we've definitely settled on the theme, have we? OK: "The Cost of Discipleship." Got it.

20

The Radio Spot

(To be placed in top 20 Christian markets Feb. 15 through March 31, as specified on attached Media Buy sheet)

If you're not employed in full time Christian work, and most of us aren't, have you ever wished that your job could count for more in God's Kingdom? Now it can, with a unique new approach to managing your money and your career. It's called ISP—that's ISP, for Income Sanctification Program. ISP will save you money and help you make each day's work count for God in new ways.

It's already worked for thousands, and it can work for you too. ISP allows you to set yourself up as a not-for-profit religious corporation, no matter what kind of work you're doing now. That's right, whether you're a butcher, a baker or a candlestick maker, you can legally enter full time ministry tomorrow—and it's all permitted by the IRS. Depending on your situation, you can save up to 40 percent on federal and state income taxes and begin taking perfectly legal deductions you aren't allowed to claim right now.

ISP is incredibly versatile, and it can work for you even if you're no longer employed and are relying only on retirement income. And, in most circumstances, it will work for you if you're in the military.

Think God might be calling you to save more money for him? Call now to learn more. We'll send you a detailed, easy to follow kit explaining how ISP works, including a DVD as well as the forms that will allow you to get into full time ministry in your state.

For only three payments of $99.95, you can begin saving hundreds or even thousands of dollars each month by follow ISP's "Ten Principles of Tax-Savvy Stewardship."

And as an added bonus, if you order today we'll also send you the "Money Matters Bible," with all verses relating to financial management highlighted in red. This elegant, leather bound gift valued at more than $50 is yours free just for ordering today. Remember, ISP comes with a 30-day money-back guarantee, so you've absolutely nothing to lose.

Call toll free 1–800-TAX-LORD—that's 1–800-TAX-LORD.

Just listen to these happy customers:

Jingle: *ISP, ISP,*
            See what the Lord has done for me.
            ISP, ISP,
            He's helping me become tax free.

Remember, that number is 1–800-TAX-LORD. Once again, 1–800-TAX-LORD.

This offer not valid in Alaska, Ohio, Puerto Rico or Wisconsin. Consult with your tax advisor or financial planner to learn how ISP applies in your situation. Amount of estimated savings will vary by state and present income level. The program is not endorsed by the IRS or any other government agency.

Bibles R Us, Inc., or, "Another Week at the Office"

Bill:

As I'll be out of the office Monday and Tuesday, I'm getting the "Weekly Possibilities" list to you a little early. Here are the top five possibilities for this week, all of which the creative team and marketing folks think have some merit. See you after my trip to Chicago.

1.   The Interior Designer Bible

2.   The Quilters Bible

3.   The Crossword Puzzler's Bible

4.   The Learning Disabilities Bible

5.   The NASCAR Bible

Aimee

No-Fault Confessions

A Bulletin Insert

As you may have heard, our parish has adopted the practice of No-Fault Confessions on a six-month trial basis. The Diocese gave us the option last March to experiment with this approach, which allows for quicker, simpler and generally less onerous confessions—for both parishioners and the priest. The great majority of those attending our town meeting last week thought that our parish should try out this option. Beginning on June 1, then, you will need to tell Fr. Tester whether you want the regular or No-Fault confession.

At next month's town hall discussion, we'll look at the possibility of extending this experiment to include on-line confessions, either via e-mail, Instant Messenger or under certain circumstances through chat rooms as well. For more information, call Cassandra in the church office.

23

Our Church is in Good Hands
With All State Insurance

"He alone is my rock and my salvation;
he is my fortress, I will never be shaken."

—PSALM 62:2

To the tune of "Away in a Manger"

Away with the danger, no risks lie ahead.
We'll win any lawsuit, our insurers have said.
Folks can sue if they want, but if you have not guessed:
When we bought our coverage, we went for the best.

So now to be prudent and avoid any fuss,
We've ended our child care and sold our church bus.
Our youth groups had also to go right away,
When our risk managers had all had their say.

Trial lawyers lie in wait, but we're quite assured.
Any possible risk is fully secured.
And it won't be long before we see the day
When for God's protection we won't need to pray.

24

SpeedyPrayer

A Software Review

This intriguingly titled program from Swiftly, Swiftly Ministries is a mixed blessing. It does much of what it promises: "make your prayer life more efficient through an easy-to-use prayer planner." Thanks to SpeedyPrayer's simple yet effective "Prayer Prioritizer," I found I could cut my daily prayer time by about a third during the 30 days I tried it out, and without any sense that I was compromising my walk with the Lord. Whether I was looking at prayers of adoration, confession, thanksgiving or supplication, I found that SpeedyPrayer delivered by helping me organize and systematize my prayer life in ways that my old 3-by-5 card system just couldn't.

As one promo for this product puts it, SpeedyPrayer allows you to use your time more effectively for the Lord's work. It's the latest in a small but highly innovative line of time management and Christian efficiency products from a vibrant dot-com company based in Boulder, Colorado. As you may know, the group of "holy nerds," as they jokingly call themselves, who run Swiftly, Swiftly Ministries were behind the highly successful RapidTithe program that came out last fall.

This latest offering doesn't have the same flexibility that RapidTithe gave hurried Christian givers. For one thing, you really ought to run this on either your laptop or desktop. It needs a far larger screen than your iPhone or Blackberry offers. But who's likely to have that laptop handy when you want to include a quick prayer when you find yourself driving by the scene of a traffic accident? Bottom line: SpeedyPrayer can work well if you confine your prayer life to one place, but for prayer warriors on the move, this program's designers need to build in much more flexibility.

SpeedyPrayer needs minimal memory, and will run equally easily on any PC or Mac. Set up is a cinch. Street price: $49.

25

A Revised Hymnody for Post-Modern Times, No. 259

Jesus loves me! This I know,
For my feelings tell me so.
I sense his love all day long;
I feel I'm right, I can't be wrong.
Refrain
Yes, Jesus loves me!
Yes, Jesus loves me!
Yes, Jesus loves me!
My feelings tell me so.

26

Speed Dating for Spiritual Seekers

It took Courtney Rees about 25 seconds to conclude that Judaism wasn't for her. And, she recalls, she needed only 15 seconds to conclude that the Baha'i faith wasn't right either. Rees' whirlwind encounter with a dozen religious traditions at Seattle's first Spirituality Speed Dating convention in fact left her with no firm commitments to any one faith, she said. But she remains intrigued by Buddhism and Roman Catholicism.

"The Buddhist monk was really cool," said Rees, a freshman at the University of Washington. "Even though we had only 90 seconds, he explained the whole thing about zen pretty well, I thought. I'll want to look into this more." The Jesuit priest who spoke with her struck her as pretty cerebral, she said, "But he used his time well to explain the richness of church tradition, and I thought that was attractive."

Rees was one of about 500 attendees at the Convention, most of them in their teens or twenties. Held last Saturday and Sunday, the event gave attendees the chance to get brief exposure to a wide range of faiths. They signed up to "speed date" up to 12 representatives of various religious traditions. The speakers, scattered in booths throughout Safeco Field, gave up to a 90-second pitch to the attendees before they had to move on to another table.

Said Mikki Nestor, director of the Greater Seattle Inter-Faith Council, "This is a great way for people who are spiritually open to get exposure to real people from a wide range of traditions, and to learn what might be a good match for them." Nestor said the event is "a low-key, fun way to learn about something that many young people want to explore; we're giving them a simple, no-commitment way to do this."

Other groups represented included several Christian traditions, such as the Southern Baptists, Mennonites and United Methodists. Hinduism was represented, as was Islam (both Sunni and Shiite traditions), secular humanism, and atheism.

Chuck Carpenter, a 26-year-old software designer, said he found the event worthwhile. "I greatly enjoyed learning about other traditions," he said. "But what I really got out of this was a chance to reconnect with my own Greek Orthodox roots. I haven't been to church in maybe 15 years, but I was amazed how much the priest could enrich me in, oh, probably no more than a minute. He was great."

Not all religious groups are comfortable with the Speed Dating approach. Rabbi Walter Liebowitz, of Tacoma, said, "It is an insult to any faith tradition to try to reduce it to a mere 90-second presentation; I didn't want to have anything to do with this."

A Moslem Imam from Seattle had a different criticism. Ali Nassam said, "I have no problem with having people describe their faith in a minute and half. But the rule that won't allow conversations to go beyond that limit is ridiculous. How can one hope to discuss things of eternal significance with a 90-second time limit?"

But the Rev. Jerry Camp, from a large independent Bible church in Los Angeles, said he was glad he had invested the time and money (all faith representatives had to pay a $250 registration fee) in the event. "I'll jump at any opportunity to present the gospel message," he said. "Ninety seconds? Hey, in that time I can give them the Four Spiritual Laws, lead them in the believer's prayer, and still have time to recite all 66 books of the Bible."

27

"It is Forbidden for God to Work Miracles Here," Updated

"By order of the King: 'It is forbidden for God to work miracles here.'" Said by an unknown wit, who wrote this comment at the entrance to a French cemetery in the time of King Louis XV. The king had closed the cemetery because of some miracles that were supposedly resulting from the relics of someone buried there.

And now, the update:

Dear God:
The Seminole Valley School Board has determined that, in keeping with Supreme Court and other legal rulings, you may no longer enter any of the schools or other facilities in the district's jurisdiction. This limitation applies both to any possible physical appearances, in the person of Jesus Christ, and to the far more common problem we have experienced, that of your Holy Spirit intruding on the district's normal operations.

I must note that the legal decisions referred to above ensure that students and district employees remain free to engage in any purely personal prayer or religious activities, providing they do not impinge on the freedom of any other individuals. However, you are forbidden from answering these prayers insofar as they may have any impact on, or in any way affect, the operations of individual schools or the district as a whole.

Should further violations occur, we shall pursue whatever actions we can against you, to the fullest extent provided by law.

Yours faithfully,
Philip Bass
President: Seminole Valley School Board

28

An Organic Pastor

"Food for the Journey," a self-described cutting edge church in Oakland, California, is advertising for a new senior pastor—with a difference. The church's ad for the position says that its new leader must be organically certified.

Carolina Pinchuk, the chair of the search committee, says, "It's part of our mission to honor the environment in every way possible. Our members have been going organic for years; that's even a requirement for anyone serving in a leadership role in our church."

So it was a logical step, she adds, to require that the church's next pastor embody this value.

Pinchuk concedes that despite the ad's wording, it won't actually be possible to find someone who is truly "organically certified."

"Our society is now evaluating virtually everything that's edible to see if it's organically grown," she says. "But we're not yet where we need to be: at the level of having an independent authority that will certify people who eat only these foods as themselves being organic."

"Until we reach that point," Pinchuk says, "we need to accept someone who will self-certify. We're OK with taking applicants at their word that they eat only organically, and are thoroughly committed to environmental causes."

The church, whose theology Pinchuk describes as "open and ecumenical but uncompromising on environmental and social issues," has about 350 members. The church's website notes it was also a pioneer in expecting its members to honor fair trade practices.

So seriously does the church take these issues that it currently has a task force exploring the theology of Jesus' use of food.

Consisting of a dozen church members, including several seminary professors, the group is looking at such issues as whether Jesus' feeding of the 5,000 honored fair trade practices, and whether his institution of the Lord's Supper meets the church's organic-only expectations.

Says Professor Arnold Beerbohm, a specialist in New Testament studies who is the task force's co-chair, "One can infer that Jesus' character and inherent purity lent to the bread and wine the organic qualities we insist upon." He adds: "But in the absence of his explicitly saying they meet these standards, how can we be sure they do? These are the kinds of important theological issues on which we need our new pastor to provide leadership."

29

The Yellow Pages

A Partial Listing

Christian Automobile Detailing—See "Automobile Detailing, Christian"
Christian Bagpipe Supplies—See "Bagpipe Supplies, Christian"
Christian Breast Enlargement—See "Breast Enlargement, Christian"
Christian Carpet Cleaning—See "Carpet Cleaning, Christian"
Christian Financial Consultants—See "Financial Consultants, Christian"
Christian Lawn Maintenance—See "Lawn Maintenance, Christian"
Christian Mental Health—See "Mental Health, Christian"
Christian Septic Tank Maintenance—See "Septic Tank Maintenance, Christian"
Christian Vacuum Cleaner Service & Repair—See "Vacuum Cleaner Service & Repair, Christian"

30

The Communion Plan

For those who have not previously celebrated the Lord's Supper with us, please note which elements are served at which stations. Ours is an inclusive community, and you are invited to choose that combination of elements* that best speaks to your health or value preferences.

Station 1:	Wine (a gentle chardonnay) and sourdough bread
Station 2:	Wine (a gentle chardonnay) and whole-wheat bread
Station 3:	Grape juice and sourdough bread
Station 4:	Grape juice and whole-wheat bread
Station 5:	Wine (a gentle chardonnay) and gluten-free bread
Station 6:	Grape juice and gluten-free bread
Station 7:	No elements served**
Station 8:	Customized combinations***

All our elements are organic and Fair Trade certified.

** *For those who feel called to show solidarity with the oppressed, who live daily with hunger and thirst. Many people choosing this option feel comfortable miming the motions of taking the elements.*

*** *For those with other preferences, who have previously arranged with the church office for their customized needs.*

31

A Sense of Occasion

When Lucy, in C. S. Lewis' "The Chronicles of Narnia" encounters Aslan the lion, she asks if he is safe. Mr. Beaver responds, "Safe? Who said anything about safe? 'Course he isn't safe. But he's good. He's the King, I tell you."

Some rules on meeting Her Majesty, Queen Elizabeth II of the United Kingdom of Great Britain and Northern Ireland:

- Stand when she enters the room.

- Shake her hand only if she offers hers to you first; shake it gently and do not pump it.

- Citizens of the United Kingdom or Commonwealth countries should bow gently on meeting her (men) or curtsey (women).

- Do not otherwise touch her, by hugging, putting your arm around her, and so on. Do not engage in other unexpected behaviors.

- Address her as "Your Majesty" when first addressing her. Thereafter, call her "Ma'am." In your final comments, you should again refer to her as "Your Majesty."

- Cell phone protocol: under no circumstances let your phone ring. Given the occasion, that is utterly inappropriate. You are, after all, in the presence of royalty.

Some rules on attending our church on Sunday:

- Come dressed as you are; we are a friendly church and want you to feel comfortable, so tank tops, shorts and flip-flops are fine.

- If you run a little late, don't worry about it; you're still most welcome.

- It's OK to bring your cup of Starbucks into worship. Donuts or other munchies are fine too.

- Getting up to take a restroom break is fine.

- Cell phone protocol: it's OK to text or check e-mails, but under no circumstances let your phone ring. Given the occasion, that is utterly inappropriate. You are, after all, in the presence of royalty.

32

The Lord's Prayer

Our Father, who art in heaven,
Hallowed be thy name.
But enough about you; now, here's my problem . . . .

33

The Senior Pastor's Difficult Phone Call, to the New Pastor of Evangelism and Outreach

Hi TJ, glad I caught you. How are things?

Good, good. The conference OK? Learning anything?

Look, I need to talk with you rather urgently about something. This isn't going to be easy. I would have preferred to wait until you got back from San Antonio, but . . . .

No, it's got nothing to do with the Jensen family; we got that all sorted out. That woman really is a whacko, isn't she?

No, it's something else, which the church council talked about at length last night and they want me to get on this right away.

Look, as I said, this isn't going to be easy for you, but I'm confident you have the grace and maturity to handle this and understand where we're coming from.

Bottom line: quite a few people on the council, well, most of them in fact, want you to pull back in your outreach efforts. Or at least refocus them.

Look TJ, you've been with us now, what, three months. And we're all thrilled with your commitment and enthusiasm and all that. But we feel you're being, how shall I put it, just a tad *too* enthusiastic.

Remember three weeks ago you brought in those two homeless guys, with their tattoos and dirty clothes. And one of them even had his shopping cart parked at the back of the church.

They didn't feel welcome, you say? Well, I would hope not.

Yes, I know what Mr. Arbuthnot told them. Actually, I'm *pleased* he told them that they wouldn't fit in at our church. From what I heard, he was very gracious about it. Firm, but gracious. And he even suggested two or three other churches where they might be more welcome.

And then there was that young woman who was all over the media when she was in that scandal with the senator. To bring someone like that into our church, to be honest, showed very poor judgment, TJ.

No, I'm not surprised she didn't return either.

You're still new here and learning our culture. And you're doing great on that, of course, but there are still some things, maybe more subtle things, you haven't picked up on yet. For example, we don't like calling people 'sinners,' at least, certainly not to their face. See, we try to be a seeker-friendly church, reaching out to people with love and a warm welcome.

To be quite blunt, we feel you're bringing in the wrong kind of people. Here's another example of poor judgment: inviting the local Socialist Party chairman to our prayer breakfast really offended a lot people. I don't know if you realized that. I mean, we're non-partisan and all that, and I don't like politics in my church, but many people spoke to me about . . . .

I understand that you thought he was at "a great point of need," as you put it. But TJ, didn't you see that he was out of place there? Nobody spoke to him, except to be polite. Even Simon Wang was upset, and he's a Democrat. And can you blame them, given the godless agenda this man has been pushing in our community? Everybody felt uncomfortable, even him.

What do you mean, "Wasn't that an opportunity to show him what we think God's agenda is?"

TJ, I think you're sort of missing my main point. As I said, we're concerned that you're bringing in the wrong kind of people.

What do I mean by "wrong kind of people"?

Well, yes, we're all sinners, of course. As you say, Jesus even invited sinners and tax collectors to join him. But what I mean is that you're drawing in the wrong kind of sinners.

What's the right kind of sinner, you ask? Well, that would be the kind of people we are equipped to minister to, of course.

For one thing, nobody wants to be made to feel like a sinner, to use your word, when they come to church. And people who will stand out because of the problems, or sins, they bring to church are going to feel shame in the presence of righteousness, not a warm welcome.

Clearly, we want them to find their place in the Kingdom of God, just like anyone else. But these kinds of people simply don't fit at First Church, TJ.

TJ, you're young, you're still learning the job. You have great gifts; you're enthusiastic. And I hope I don't sound patronizing when I say this, TJ, but you still need to learn some hard realities of ministry—like the fact that homeless people and these other marginal types won't pay the heating bills. That may not be something they teach you in seminary, but that's reality.

I'm glad you understand. Good. OK, I probably need to get to the staff meeting.

What's that? A new idea you want to run by the church council and me? Sure, we can talk more when you get back. But you'd like me to think about it in the meantime?

An outreach program to convicted sex offenders in the community, you say?

34

An Imagined Response
to Tony Campolo's Bad Word

Tony Campolo is an author and a popular, if at times provocative, speaker on Christian college campuses. For example, writer John Oliver Mason noted in a profile on Campolo: "At times he would tell an audience, 'I have three things I'd like to say today. First, while you were sleeping last night, 30,000 children died of starvation or diseases related to malnutrition. Second, most of you don't give a shit.' Then he would add, 'What's worse is that you're more upset with the fact that I said shit than the fact that 30,000 kids died last night.'"

Dear Mr. Campolo:

It is with both a heavy heart and deep anger that I write to you, following your remarks in our campus chapel last Wednesday.

I speak on behalf of our campus and Board of Trustees when I say that as an invited guest to our Christian community, you grossly violated our hospitality. Your foul language contaminated a sacred place, where we have faithfully worshipped a holy God since our college's founding 82 years ago. Your reckless grandstanding and shameful rhetorical device prevented the hundreds of students and faculty in attendance from hearing whatever your message may have been.

Many of our students were so distraught at what you said that our chaplain and counselors in the health center have been overwhelmed by visits from those unable to reconcile such language with someone who is supposedly a man of God.

By return of mail, I expect an explicit, unqualified apology for your outrageous conduct. And be assured that in the meantime an entire college community is now praying for your spiritual wellbeing.

Most disappointedly yours,
Arthur J. Fenster—President

P.S.: Another thing: I did some checking and learned that the World Health Organization estimates that an average of only 27,350 children die each day. As a Christian academic community we are confident enough that because all truth is God's truth, we see no need to distort or embellish the facts. Unlike you, apparently.

Copies: The Board of Trustees
          All faculty and staff (via e-mail)
          All students (via e-mail)
          All local and state media (via e-mail)
          Posted to college website

35

The Very Model

I am the very model of a multi-tasking parish priest.
I work on many tasks at once, but always three or four at
  least.
My efficiency has tripled since I started multi-tasking,
And my strategies I gladly share, they're yours just for the
  asking.

Each day I start with prayer and study, and update my daily
  plan.
Every moment is so precious, I squeeze in all the tasks I can.
I twitter and I text by phone and I send e-mails by the score;
I strive to touch a hundred souls before I'm even out the
  door.

At the parish office I start the tasks of administration;
These are quickly tackled by some expeditious delegation.
My schedule always is on Outlook, in clear five-minute col-
  ored blocks;
Each day I plan for everything, down to the color of my
  socks.

I am perfectly obsessive about the ways I use my time;
When preparing my homily and thinking pastoral thoughts
  sublime,

I'm checking my favorite Websites for updates on sports and
stocks and news.
I'll also add to my own blog, expounding for the world my
views.

I use three cell phones all at once and I even text while
preaching.
I'll be deep in meditation when people think I am teaching.
I have my parish so well trained and organized to the extent,
The ill and frail know they can't die without my knowledge
and consent.

Multi-tasking has its dangers, of that there's surely little
doubt.
Priests and pastors overdo it and all too many can burn out.
So in combining two more things, I'm at my multi-tasking
best:
For seventeen hours straight I work, on this my Sabbath day
of rest.

(With apologies to Gilbert and Sullivan)

36

Suffer the Little Children to Come Unto Me

Dear Jesus:

Thank you for your recent application for the part-time job in our church nursery. I need to tell you that the selection committee easily identified you as our top candidate, given your clear love of children and your extraordinarily powerful way of connecting with them.

Unfortunately, your criminal background check by the State Highway Patrol revealed a felony conviction for sedition. As you may be aware, our zero-tolerance policy against hiring convicted felons prevents us from considering you further for this position.

Perhaps you will find other areas where you can find an outlet for your obvious people skills and great heart for ministry. One of the hiring committee suggested you consider linking with a ministry for work-release prisoners; given your own experience with the criminal justice system, this may be a fruitful area of service for you.

But I am afraid we see no future for you in working with children, either professionally or as a volunteer.

All the best as you seek to minister elsewhere,

Most sincerely,
Claudia K. Grassley
Chair—Children's Ministries

37

The Day the Donut Man Didn't Show

Nobody ever learned why the donut man didn't show up before the first service on Sunday, May 13. But, looking back, all the members at Grace Fellowship knew this was the catalyst for everything that followed.

The problem emerged at about 9:10 that morning, when Mrs. Lunscomb noticed the standing order of five dozen assorted donuts hadn't yet arrived. The donut man always had them there by 9 sharp, in ample time for the fellowship hour at the end of the first service, which typically ended at 9:30.

But Mrs. Lunscomb had been paired for fellowship hour ministry that morning with Mrs. Phillips. Nobody who had even half a brain or had been around Grace Fellowship for more than a month or two would make that mistake. Unfortunately, with the church secretary having been ill with the Swine flu, the woman from the temporary agency could not have known that she was putting together two deeply spiritual but utterly incompatible saints, who simultaneously loathed and loved each other in a way that only Christians can understand.

When Mrs. Lunscomb pointed out to Mrs. Phillips that the donuts hadn't arrived, she added that with twenty minutes to go, they would probably still show up.

On the contrary, said Mrs. Phillips. Knowing how reliable the donut man always was, there was surely some problem. Also, it would be better to be safe than sorry, and she thought she should go to the store right away for a backup supply.

The tone of the exchange was testy, not surprising in the light of their long antagonism.

"We should just wait, Becky," said Mrs. Lunscomb. "I'm sure they'll show up."

"I'm afraid I disagree, dear," replied Mrs. Phillips. "I'd hate to see the disappointment on those little ones' faces if we don't have any donuts for them."

They went back and forth for another four or five minutes, with testiness quickly advancing to full-fledged, forced-smile hostility. Mrs. Phillips then proclaimed, "I'm sorry, but it's now 9:15 and I don't think we can take the chance that they'll still arrive." She then picked up her purse from under the table, a shade more vigorously than normal. With twelve steps, which somehow conveyed irritation, superiority and self-righteousness all at the same time, she headed out of the fellowship hall, toward the parking lot, on her rescue mission.

Already hurt and slighted, Mrs. Lunscomb, was now for the first time afraid that the donuts may indeed not arrive. She was also a little embarrassed, as she realized that Donut Man might be ill, or have been in an accident, so she belatedly said a quick prayer for his well being, and a safe delivery of donuts.

But the prayer didn't yield any donuts and, at 9:28, when she heard the congregation singing the doxology, she was on the verge of panic. Then the four Sutcliffe children burst into the fellowship hall, and, as was their long-standing habit, headed straight to what was now a still-empty donut table.

Three-year-old Krissy Sutcliffe cried, "Where are the donuts?" Mrs. Lunscomb got about five words into a stumbling explanation when she was drowned out by Krissy's howling. Her three siblings joined her and the Sutcliffe children soon sounded like a quartet of surprisingly youthful professional mourners.

That's when Mrs. Sutcliffe lit into Mrs. Lunscomb, demanding to know the whereabouts of the donuts. Other parents, by now trying to contain their crying children too, also joined in, demanding an explanation. Yet others, trying to rise above the chaos, tried yelling that there must be some reasonable explanation for the absent donuts and that, in any event, it was hardly Mrs. Lunscomb's fault. Mrs. Lunscomb tried explaining that Becky Phillips had gone to get extras and should be back any minute.

By now, she too was in tears, stunned by the turn of events over which she had no control, and retreated to the kitchen to compose herself. Mrs. Wilkens stood next to her, with her hand on Mrs. Lunscomb's shoulder, repeatedly saying "I know, I know," between her sobs.

In the fellowship hall itself, the fray continued, with parents and other donut seekers engaging in heated debates over where the donuts might be, and whose fault it was that the time of fellowship had been disrupted.

Suddenly, cheers erupted as Mrs. Phillips staggered back into the hall, hardly able to see over the stack of donut boxes she bore triumphantly, like the Israelites' desperately needed manna and quail, toward the empty tables.

But if the children's cries quickly ended, the adults' arguments over what went wrong, and who was responsible for what, did not.

Even as the children munched, Pastor Kennedy sensed a tension among the grownups that he had never before seen in his thirteen years at Grace Fellowship. He hoped matters would soon settle down, but his instincts warned him otherwise.

He was right: quickly, the church solidified into two factions. One group thought Mrs. Lunscomb had grossly neglected her duties, both by dismissing Mrs. Phillips' quest for an assured donut supply, and by abandoning her station at the donut table when she was most needed to handle the crisis. At the very least, this group said, she could have done something to alert the congregation to the missing donuts, and enable parents to prepare the children for this news. (A young man in this faction who was studying to be a paralegal kept referring to Mrs. Lunscomb's responsibility to "mitigate damages" in these circumstances.)

The other group took Mrs. Lunscomb's side, saying that she had done all that was expected of her. Moreover, it was increasingly clear to this group that others were attacking her because she had strongly opposed a controversial new policy that the church leadership had recently adopted. No longer could groups or individuals outside the church use the church kitchen for catering events. Things came to a head when the Katzenbach family, who had left the church, on good terms, two years earlier for a much smaller church, wanted to use Grace Fellowship's sizable fellowship hall (and kitchen) for their 50th wedding anniversary. They were turned down because of the new policy. The decision angered many in the church and Mrs. Lunscomb was one of the most vocal critics.

Soon, each side was demanding apologies from the other, with Mrs. Lunscomb having become a human piñata between the two groups. It therefore came as no surprise that a special church meeting was called to address what was more and more obviously a growing rift in the church. Initially, Pastor Kennedy had sought to calm down both sides, striving desperately to stay neutral. But each faction began to take strong stands and brought into the open other controversial issues in the church (which curriculum to use in the Sunday School, what precise mix of traditional and contemporary music to have at the 11 a.m. service, and so on).

After getting more and more explicit and implicit messages from his flock "that you are either with us or against us, Pastor," the Rev. Kennedy found himself in the end forced to ally with one group or the other. He chose the traditionalists.

Mrs. Lunscomb and her family left the church, along with about a third of the membership. And two years later, just when Pastor Kennedy thought healing of his remnant congregation was finally taking hold, he in turn was ousted, over a dispute about who should design the banners for the Easter service.

Rather than seek a new pastorate, he concluded he was burned out from the ministry and took early retirement at age 62. He now spends his days reading, playing golf and delighting in his four grandchildren, all of whom live in town. He and his extended family now attend a different church. During this church's coffee hour on Sundays, Pastor Kennedy was relieved to notice the first time he visited, no donuts are served.

38

The Church's One Foundation (Updated)

The Church's one foundation,
Is Jesus Christ her Lord.
He is our brand and trademark,
Like Apple, Coke or Ford.
The cross serves as our logo,
A sign we gladly bear.
It sets the church apart
And boosts our market share.

In a very crowded market,
Where many faiths contend,
We have our own true savior,
The Son whom God did send.
We'll stay a market leader,
For God has wisely planned;
In his great love he gave us,
Lord Jesus as our brand.

39

The Invoice

Healings Are Us

June 17

To: Mary, Martha & Lazarus Anderson

Dear Mesdames & Sir:

Final Notice
I am once again submitting our invoice, No. 3496, for services rendered last February 23. I must point out that this account is now more than 90 days past due. As you know, your medical insurance carrier has rejected your claim, describing this resurrection event as experimental treatment. You are therefore responsible for the full amount due.

I have received your letter dated April 2, in which you say that you understand this service was provided "as a personal favor by Jesus of Nazareth, who is a family friend." Mr. Alvarez, our financial manager, has authorized me, as a goodwill gesture, to charge you a discounted rate for the services that Jesus of Nazareth provided you. I am afraid the other items are fixed expenses and are not discountable.

If this revised amount is not paid by June 30, we shall be forced to turn this amount over to a collection agency.

The original invoice is reprinted below for your convenience.

For Professional Services

Raising Lazarus from the Dead (at courtesy discounted rate)	$3,250.00
Professional Weeping	$355.00
Attending Disciples (12 Disciples at $155/hour, for 2 hours)	$310.00
Travel to and from Jerusalem	$278.00
Accommodation and meals	$216.00
Emergency surcharge	$250.00
Subtotal	**$4,659.00**
Roman Taxing Officer Assessment (8%)	$373.72
TOTAL	**$5031.72**

Yours sincerely,
Annabelle Simpson
Accounts Payable

40

How Prayers Get Answered

"Thank you Jesus for bringing Kia to our town." This sign was erected in the town of West Point, Georgia, July 2009, after the Kia auto company decided to build a $1.2 billion plant in this economically struggling community of about 3,500.

"OK, Gabriel. So what do we have on the agenda for today?"

"Your Father would like you to relocate Microsoft from Washington State to Arkansas. The folks in Arkansas are really hurting in this economy, as you know, and could use the help. It will come as an answer to the prayers of many Arkansans."

"Have they specifically been praying to get Microsoft?"

"No, but this would be a more general answer to their prayers."

"What will that do to the people in Washington?"

"Well, it'll be a real surprise to Bill Gates and his crowd, that's for sure. But your Father says the people of Washington will be OK. For some of them, He says, it will turn them back to prayer. Anyway, it's His will that they move."

"Of course. What else?"

"Your Father wants that major Department of Defense contract to go to Northrop Grumman, even though its bid is considerably higher than those of its two competitors."

"And that's answering the prayers of some Christians working for Northrop Grumman, right?"

"Yes, Lord. It will have all kinds of political repercussions, but as your Father likes to say, that's not our problem."

"Right. Anything else?"

"One other item, Lord. It's a particularly tricky one. Your Father wants to respond to a whole bunch of conflicting prayers about something called the Super Bowl."

41

Jesus Does Stand-Up

By entertainment reporter Liz Potts

"Son of God . . ." "Savior . . ." "King of Kings . . . " "The Messiah . . ." Those are just some of the things they're saying about Jesus of Galilee, the new stand-up comic who's pulling in large audiences with a patter that arises out of his unique religious ministry. Well, he may be all those things, and more. But what really matters is, can he entertain us? The short answer is, "You bet!"

Jesus is the latest in a long line of Jewish comedians, like Lenny Bruce, Henny Youngman and Woody Allen. As this young Galilean says, "What do you expect, I'm a Jew: I do comedy." He adds, "You need to reach people where they're at. I mean, that's what my incarnation is all about, isn't it? What more profound way is there for God to relate to people? And it's the same with my comedy. It's all about connecting with people, right?"

But this articulate young Galilean is the most unlikely of comedians. For one thing, he's steeped in theology, and superb in out-arguing hecklers who try to trip him up, which gets even more laughs from the crowd.

"Yes, people need to hear my good news of salvation. But they need entertainment too," Jesus says. "Let's face it: who doesn't prefer a good laugh to yet another sermon? I could Twitter my Sermon on the Mount a thousand times and it won't have the same impact as getting a comedy club audience laughing—and then getting my message across."

Let's look at an excerpt from one of his monologues, performed last month at the Luminous Mango Club, in Milwaukie, Wisconsin. Opening for him that evening were "The Twelve Disciples," his regular warm-up group whose slapstick act is hilarious: they get everything wrong, try walking on water, ask Jesus inane questions, and pretend to run away if they get frightened. Then comes the one they call the Teacher . . .

Hi there, how's everyone doing tonight? Good? If not, I can fix that, you know.

(Laughter)

Like you, sir, up front, you with the crutches. See me after the show and we'll see what I can do, OK? And feel free to laugh, OK? I mean, really loud. And long, and hard. No need to worry: if anyone next to you dies laughing, just let me know. I can fix it.

(Laughter)

But seriously, folks, this healing thing is really tricky. Take today, for example. I was in Bethsaida and ran into this guy who was blind. Couldn't see a thing. I guess that's why I ran into him; he couldn't see me coming. But I'm a healer. I mean, that's what I do. So I get some spit and rub it on this guy's eyes. That's what I usually do. Spit's great stuff. You've always got some with you, right?

(Laughter)

Anyway, I know the medical people might say this is experimental treatment—not an approved therapeutic intervention, and all that, but it's worked plenty of times for me. But not today. This time, the guy tells me, "I can see people walking but they look like trees." I mean, what a bummer. So he can't yet see properly. If he'd said, "I can see people but they all look like Angelina Jolie," that's a problem most guys wouldn't mind having.

(Laughter)

But trees? Poor guy. He's been blind for years and the first thing he sees is people who look like trees. He's really polite about it. Doesn't complain. Doesn't ask for a second opinion or anything. But I can tell he's real disappointed. And I'm like, "God, are you trying to tell me something here?" Anyway, I try again and this time he sees everything clearly. So I point to a tree and I ask him what he sees. And he says, "Zacchaeus."

(Laughter)

No, just kidding. He'd only sneezed. Sure sounded like "Zacchaeus" though. Then he takes a look at my disciples, and says, "You know, I think I prefer the trees."

(Laughter)

But this blindness is a strange thing. I keep meeting blind people. And not just the physically blind. The spiritually blind are even worse. And the worst are the Pharisees. Curing them? Now that's really hard work. You know why? They're all walking round with these planks in one eye, and dust specks in the other. I dunno what it is with these planks. Maybe it's some secret society thing. Like Freemasons. You join the Greater Galilee Pharisees Club and they give you this plank, and you shove it into your eye.

(Laughter)

I mean, couldn't they have come up with something simpler to show they're members, like a button or a secret handshake? Anyway, these guys are going round, with these planks in their eyes, and having a terrible time. Imagine taking your driving test, with this plank sticking out of your eye. Or being on a date and chatting up this girl. A real conversation stopper. Especially if you're on a blind date.

(Laughter)

I don't know if you're allowed to take the plank out at night, when you go to sleep. Otherwise, it's "Good night, dear," give your wife a kiss, and it's thwack, you slap her in the face yet again. And no matter how long you've been married, with the lights out she still doesn't see it coming.

(Laughter)

You've been a great audience. But I've got to run. I've got a whole bunch of Medicare reimbursements to try and figure out before President Obama gives me any more change I can believe in.

(Laughter)

Thank you so much, thank you, thank you.

(Laughter and applause)

42

An Exciting Time at Our Savior's College

"'Everything is permitted' in our Lotus-land of free-
dom. The result of our casual nihilism is a careless
demolition of tradition and the creation of a spiritu-
al, moral and aesthetic wasteland in its place—not
only in society but also in the church."

—Os Guinness

Dear Alumni, Supporters, Students, Faculty, Staff and other friends of Our Savior's:

It is with great excitement that I share with you the culmination of our two-year "Vision 20/20" planning process, which has led us to adopt a series of bold initiatives endorsed by the Board of Trustees at their meeting last week.

Many of you know that when I was appointed president of Our Savior's three years ago, the Board set as my highest priority the need to develop a new ten-year plan. And here we have it!

If I can summarize this 240-page document in one sentence, it is that "the new Our Savior's College will in the next decade transcend its Christian roots and became an even more inclusive and an even richer academic community." You can access the full "Vision 20/20" report on our website.

What this means in practical terms is that we will now intentionally recruit faculty from other faith traditions, and even those from no faith traditions at all, as we seek to enrich our community of learning. In practice, this is not a major change, as we have for a long while not enforced our earlier requirement that faculty submit a faith statement, which we have found stifling and counter-productive in getting the strongest faculty we can.

Moreover, this inclusiveness of all faith perspectives more accurately reflects who we have become as a community: a community proud of its religious tradition but one that also repudiates the narrowness and intolerance of creedal or sectarian views.

Our students will soon experience several other tangible benefits. We will scrap our embarrassingly outdated visitation policies in the dorms, as we will seek in future to incorporate into our life together those values that our students themselves endorse. Likewise, our mandatory once-a-week chapel attendance, understandably long unpopular, will be replaced by optional "journey exploration" discussions in the dorms. (This program will be overseen by the new inter-faith chaplain whom we plan to hire this summer.)

In the curriculum, the last remaining Biblical literature requirement required of all students will be replaced (can you just hear that sigh of relief from around campus!) by one of three options. One is an innovative interdisciplinary course examining the Christian faith, titled "The Church: A Fearful Hegemony." Another option is a course in world faith traditions. The third choice is for students to undertake an independent project with a non-profit organization, as part of our new "Helping Others Helps Me" service learning program.

The Board and I are convinced that strategically too this is a wise move for Our Savior's, as we increasingly seek to appeal to prospective students who are uncomfortable with the narrower and, to be candid, often intellectually limiting educational environments that many more traditionally religious schools provide.

As you may have heard, especially from some of our more vocal alumni, not everyone has bought into what I see as an exhilarating vision for the future. The Vision 20/20 document also contains a dissenting minority report, written by three task force members who strongly objected to "abandoning our Christian identity," as they put it. To his great credit, the task force chair insisted, in the interest of fairness, on including this dissenting voice, even though the chair and I agree that its alarmist language and anti-change attitudes make it difficult to take seriously this small group's concerns. I'm sure you'll agree if you read the dissent that it offers a well-intentioned but nevertheless reactionary, backward-looking perspective.

My profound thanks to our Vision 20/20 task force for their extraordinary efforts and commitment to envisioning an exciting future for Our Savior's. I am humbled that I will have the privilege of helping our college move in that direction. Much work lies ahead for all of us. An immediate task, on which I invite your ideas and suggestions, will be taken up by the committee I have just appointed to determine a new name for Our Savior's that better reflects who we are and what we want to become.

Warmly,
President Bev Leith
Copy: Board of Trustees

43

The "Second Coming" Dispute Enters Mediation

The three-week-old strike by a group of Christians who have "downed tools" against God is heading to mediation. The federal government has ordered the two sides to meet to try to resolve their differences over the return of Jesus Christ. The first mediation session begins in Philadelphia tomorrow.

Concerned Christians for the Second Coming, or CCSC, welcomed the talks, saying in a news release that "this promising development may help us to get from God what we have not been able to obtain through faithful and patient prayer."

CCSC launched the strike on May 14, after God failed to meet the group's deadline for Christ to return. At that point, CCSC's president, the Rev. Rob Finch, said that he and the CCSC board agreed it was time to force God's hand. They called for all their supporters and "other God-fearing believers to go on strike." Since then, Finch says, millions of Christians have refused to pray, read their Bibles, attend church, share their faith with friends or anything else they believe might further God's kingdom.

Finch added, "Christians in the United States today are under siege from a coalition of secular, socialist and humanistic forces. We need all the help we can get from God, and our group has been praying faithfully for years asking Him to hasten his return."

In earlier statements CCSC had also insisted that God make two changes to the original Ten Commandments: adjusting the Second Commandment to specify that the United Nations and world government are idols, and adding a commandment forbidding any teaching of evolutionary theory. But following fierce infighting with CCSC's leadership these demands were dropped in favor of concentrating only on the "second coming" demand, said one senior CCSC source who asked not to be identified.

While it is unclear what the mediation might yield, some observers say that God's negotiating team will be unwilling to concede any ground. One of the members of God's team, who arrived in Philadelphia today, said, "Scripture makes it plain that the timing of the second coming is God's business. These CCSC people have to be kidding themselves if they think God is going to yield to their agenda." Asking not to be identified because of the sensitivity of the situation, he added, "As God said to Moses, 'Is the Lord's arm too short?' These guys don't have a clue who they're arm wrestling with."

44

Death Loses its Sting
at Conestoga Chapel by the Lake

Just a stylebook reminder for all of you submitting material for the church newsletter, posting items to the church website, and so on. We're still getting many items that aren't following the church Stylebook and Policy Manual on the topic of "death." For your convenience, here's the entry once again. You can refer to the full manual on the church website.

Death and Dying: We do not use these words or directly related terms in any written or spoken material. The pastoral team doesn't use them in any of their sermons or other communications; nor should the rest of us. Many in our church find references to these concepts painful in the extreme, especially during a season of grief or other times of high vulnerability. As you know, the approximately 2,300 people affiliated with our church in some way or another are at various stages in their spiritual journeys. The concept of "death" or "dying" can be troubling to those unsure of their faith, or people who are in a pre-faith status. And for people outside the church, any references to "death" during a memorial service can be unsettling indeed.

At the risk of sounding irreverent, it's true to say that people "no longer die" at Conestoga Chapel by the Lake.

Acceptable alternatives to this term are "passing" or "passed on," "gone to glory," "resting in Jesus' arms," "entered into heavenly rest," or "entered into eternal rest." These latter three terms are especially suitable in situations following a long illness.

Avoid terms like "resting in Abraham's bosom." Many people struggle with the word "bosom," and many others don't know who "Abraham" is.

For those involved in worship services or other occasions that may require the reading of a Bible passage, please note that in keeping with the pastoral team's wishes we also need to use appropriate substitutions for the words "death," "dying," "dead," and so on. In these situations, please use good judgment in making substitutions. For example, if you were to read "Where, O death, is your victory? Where, O death, is your sting?" a suitable paraphrased substitution might be: "Where, O great leveler, is your victory? Where, O great leveler, is your sting?"

If in doubt, please seek advice from Pastor Edmonds or the associate pastors.

On a related note, we do not conduct "funerals" at our church. Please do not use that term. The pastors will perform only memorial services or, our preferred term "life celebrations." Although not a style question as such, please note too that we will under no circumstances permit a service when an actual casket is present (please note that the word "coffin" is never used; it is far too morbid). Ours is a seeker-friendly church, and nothing is more off-putting either to regular attendees or visitors than having a casket in the sanctuary.

45

The Christmas Accommodation Crunch

"There is one test, and one only, of the extent of our love for [Jesus], and it is a very uncomfortable one. How have we handled the poor?"

—Michael Green

Except for Jem Tinker, the custodian, the church was deserted on that Wednesday afternoon. He was doing last-minute cleaning before the frenzy of the Christmas eve services tomorrow. At about 4:15 he saw them: a homeless couple, a man and, probably, his aging mother. They were grubby and looked tired.

"Can I help you?" asked Jem.

The man spoke: "Hi there. We're from out of town and need a place to sleep over Christmas. Can you help?"

Jem said: "Sorry, we don't have anything here. We sometimes host something called the Interfaith Hospitality Network."

He caught himself just in time and instead of saying "homeless," he continued: "We provide beds for people who need a place. But it's not our turn this week. I think the Methodists are doing it over Christmas. Or maybe the Jewish temple, I'm not sure. Sometimes they like to give the churches a break over Christmas."

"I see," the man said. For the first time Jem noticed that the woman looked gray with exhaustion.

"Won't you sit down," Jem said, gesturing to one of the easy chairs in the lobby. The man took her arm, directed her to the chair. He turned to Jem and said, "Thank you."

After a short pause, he spoke again: "Do you have any other ideas? Anything else you can think of?"

Jem knew the church's policy: there was no way he could let them stay on the premises. Yet he felt compelled, especially as he looked at the woman in the chair, with her eyes shut and her head tilted back, to let her rest awhile.

If only to buy time, and at least show this couple that he was sensitive to their plight, he said: "Tell you what, let me call the pastor and see if he has any suggestions."

The man replied, without any noticeable reaction, "OK. Thanks."

Jem deliberately called from the courtesy phone in the lobby, so the couple could hear his side of the conversation.

Pastor Wygand answered right away. Fortunately, the couple didn't hear his wary tone, which was the result of having lived through countless Christmas crises during his 27 years of ministry.

After Jem explained the need, Pastor Wygand resisted the temptation to chide the custodian for not doing what he should have: turn these people away.

Nor could the couple hear what he told Jem: "I'm sorry, Jem. We can't help. There's nothing we can do. Ask Bob Nunn. He runs the Scotsman Inn. Maybe he has a room he can let them have. Here, let me get you Bob's number. But they'll struggle to find a room anywhere over Christmas."

He added, "I can't think of anyone else in the church who could help. You know, we can't expect our people to take in a couple of complete strangers."

Then, his mind jumped forward to the sermon he would deliver three times tomorrow night, about the out-of-towners who showed up in Bethlehem 2,000 years ago. He felt a surge of embarrassment and guilt.

He gave a short, nervous laugh and asked Jem, "She's not nine months pregnant or anything, is she? We're not talking about Mary and Joseph here, are we?" Another short laugh.

"No, pastor."

"Try phoning Bob and if he can't help, just tell them there's nothing we can do." Jem took down Bob Nunn's number.

"Thanks. You have a good day, pastor." He hung up.

He turned back to the couple. The man was standing by the woman, who still had her eyes shut and her head tilted back. She could even have been asleep by now.

"There's one thing the pastor suggested," Jem said. "A guy in our church has a motel and maybe he has a room he can let you have."

The man said, "The Scotsman Inn?"

Jem asked, "How did you know?"

"Oh, someone at another church suggested that. But they were full."

Jem didn't know what to say. He glanced at the woman. Her eyes were still shut.

The man said, "Not to worry. You've been very kind. I'm sure we'll find something." He turned to the woman and said, "Mom, we need to go."

She opened her eyes, and with a resignation that came from who knows how many other rejections that day, she got to her feet with the man's help. The two of them turned and headed toward the exit.

The man turned back and said, "Thank you, Jem. Thanks for trying."

Jem nodded. Inexplicably, he had a lump in his throat as he saw this couple leave. It was only half an hour later that he realized there was no way the man could have known his name.

That was long after the man and his mother walked down the path cutting through the church's meticulously manicured front lawn.

Then Mary spoke: "Son, why do you always want to travel at Christmas? But you've been like that since before you were born, I suppose."

Jesus replied. "We need to keep testing them, Mom. One of these years they'll get it right. Only two more churches, and then we'll head home."

46

Lazarus and his HMO

Yes, yes, I can hold.

I'm still here, yes. My patient ID? Let's see, here it is: 396045.

I'd like an appointment, with my regular doctor, please. Dr. Nichol.

Oh. When did he leave?

OK, well Dr. Figuera would be just fine.

No, nothing in particular. It's just for a checkup. A general physical.

Well, no, there's nothing wrong right now. It's just that I had this, well, unusual experience. I died, you see, and was brought back to . . . .

Yes, I said I died.

Yes, I was dead. Was dead for three days, buried, stone in front of the tomb, wrapped up in bandages. The whole thing.

No ma'am, I'm not messing you around.

And no, I've not had any concussions recently.

No, I've not been drinking. No drugs either, that's right.

And no history of mental illness. Look, with all respect, Ma'am, you're the appointment scheduler, not a consulting nurse, OK?

Just yesterday. That's when I was resurrected. I died last Thursday.

Now? Well, I'm mostly fine. A bit stiff, and I'm still trying to get used to daylight.

No, I'm not trying to be funny.

No, it wasn't a *near* death experience; it was an *actual* death experience. Lady, I should know: I was there.

Well, yes, I suppose it is unusual to get a call like this.

What did I die of? I don't know, actually. It was something fever-related, but it happened quickly, I honestly don't know.

But now I'd like to see a doctor, as I said. After what I've been through, I just thought a checkup would be a good idea. Can't be too careful, that's what I say.

Yes, Dr. Figuera, that's fine. I've seen him before, he's great. No, I'm sure I don't want a referral to a psychiatrist. Quite sure, thank you.

What do you mean, you'll have to get back to me?

You don't believe me, do you?

Yes, I suppose I'm not your typical caller, with "snots or sneezes or a boil on my butt," as you so elegantly put it. Well, then, can I speak to your supervisor, please?

OK, I'll hold.

What a pain. I bet her boss will give me the same run around. I'm just a number to these people. If someone well known called and told them they'd been raised from the dead, then they'd listen. Like Herod, or Pilate or Caesar. Or Jesus. They'd believe him.

Hello? Yes, as I was telling your colleague . . . .

47

Today's Sunday School Offerings

Vicki Frost, from Tennessee, was one of several Christians who in the mid-1980s sued the school district in which her daughter was enrolled. The case received national attention. Among her concerns were that the schools not expose her daughter to the teaching of evolution, anything critical of the free enterprise system (because "capitalism is ordained by God") or reading about Catholicism, which she said could confuse her daughter's thinking. She also opposed teaching of "the metric system, which," she said, "promotes 'one-world' government."

Good morning everyone. Welcome to worship, this first Sunday in September. And a special welcome to all you students from the college. It's great to have you here. Just one important announcement before we begin our service today. I want to remind you that our adult Sunday School classes also begin this morning. They're listed in the bulletin but I want to highlight them briefly.

Professor Mark Bunsen, from the college, will teach a course on "Time Zones and the International Date Line: The Biblical View." As some of you know, Professor Bunsen is an expert on these secular challenges to our faith. Some of you have read his latest book, "The Metric System and a Christian America: The Continuing Threat."

And our associate pastor, Craig Flannery, is teaching, "'No' to Taxes: Unexpected Lessons from Lamentations."

And lastly, for those you who are history buffs, you might be interested in a great session taught by Vern Lancaster. You'll learn how the thinking of the early church fathers and that of other figures like John Calvin and Martin Luther all reveal the church's support from the beginning for an anti-flag burning amendment.

Great options, all of them. Let me encourage you to take advantage of them. Now, let's turn to our call to worship.

48

The Jesus Squad

Jessica Towers is one of millions of Christians around the country who take seriously the prospect of Christ's second coming. But in addition to trying to lead a holy, God-fearing life until that moment arrives, Towers has brought her own take on preparing for that moment: For the past four years, she's directed a cheerleading squad whose sole task is to prepare routines to welcome Jesus back.

"We want to be ready for this unprecedented moment," says Towers, a camping equipment sales representative in Amarillo, Texas. "And what better way to have a cheerleading team on hand to herald this instant that will culminate all of history."

Modeled loosely on the legendary Dallas Cowboys Cheerleaders, Towers' 24-strong team calls itself "The Jesus Squad."

The squad practices about six hours a week. Towers says, "We've got a great bunch of gals who love Jesus but who also love to have fun and, if things work out, want to be on hand and in uniform to usher in our Lord's return."

The cheerleaders are all between 18 and 24. Towers decided, quite arbitrarily, she admits, on these age limits. "We want to convey an image of youthful yet nevertheless adult beauty," she says. "The gals understand that when they turn 25 they'll be dropped from the program, but many of them continue to support us in other ways," she adds, like helping with the training, making the team's distinctive costumes (purple to honor Jesus' royal status), or assisting with fundraising.

The squad's limited budget allows for little of the pampering that's part of the Dallas Cowboys Cheerleaders' way of doing things. There's no high-end hair care, make-up or cosmetic dental care. But they set a priority on nurturing their tans year round.

Unlike their Dallas counterparts, the women give no public performances, Towers says. "We rehearse for an audience of only one Person," she adds. "It's just we have no idea when he might show up." Like everyone associated with the program, Towers will describe their routines only in vague generalities: "They're very much like the routines you'd see at any football match, except that everything we do is cheering on Jesus and his return."

One of the team members is 22-year-old Ruth Krapeski, a receptionist in a pediatrician's office. She has been on the squad for four years, she says. "If the Lord tarries, I'll be able to serve another two years," she says. Is she bothered by the fact that she may have committed six years to practicing for a performance that may never occur while she's on the squad? "Not a bit," she responds. "This is all for God's glory, whether people see it or not."

What of criticisms that Jesus could return at a time when the women aren't all together, practicing their drills? Towers isn't fazed. "Of course we don't know the hour of our Lord's return." She adds: "People may be all over town, or even out of town. But we've thought this through and have all ready to go a system using text messages, e-mail alerts and a phone tree to get everyone together." The team even practices trying to assemble a basic squad as quickly as possible, in what they call "Jumpin' for Jesus" drills. Towers says that thanks to careful cross-training, the squad can perform its basic routines with as few as 16 members.

"Our best Jumpin' for Jesus time so far has been 33 minutes," says Krapeski. "And that's with us all suited up, the music ready to go, and everything."

Nor is Towers uncomfortable about answering this question: Doesn't the whole cheerleading program assume that Jesus, out of all the places he could choose, will physically return to Amarillo, a city of about 200,000?

"We're acting in faith here," she says. "Is it possible that Jesus may choose another location? Sure. Maybe even likely. Obviously, we can't know where, exactly, he'll return."

But she continues, "We must remember that the Lord's return will be surrounded in mystery. Maybe he'll somehow miraculously appear everywhere at once, to all his people, or somehow all believers will be gathered together in one place. We don't know."

But what she does know, she insists, is that "We're called to be ready, and however and whenever God decides to do this, we'll have a set of uniforms pressed and a set of routines ready to roll."

49

Yet Another Rejection

Dear Mr. Yahweh:

Thank you for the opportunity to consider your manuscript, "The Bible." We have read the work in-house and also sought the opinion of two outside readers. Regrettably, all who have examined the manuscript agree that it is seriously deficient in many respects, and falls well short of publishable standards.

The readers' concerns were significant and numerous, and space permits me to highlight only a few of the most important weaknesses they identified. To be blunt, the entire point of the manuscript is unclear; the thesis is jumbled, unfocused and extremely hard to detect. The structure you have chosen—dividing the book into two main sections, with 39 "books" in the first and another 27 in the second, seems needlessly complex and confusing. Also, the inexplicable mix of genres and styles within these works left our readers bewildered.

Clearly, the work has some merit. "Occasional flashes of brilliant literary style," said one of our readers. "At times, the writer shows a great gift of narrative," said another, who added: "The manuscript at times reflects an astonishing understanding of the human condition."

But offsetting these and other strengths were complaints about a "hopelessly unorganized and impossible to understand plot," "massive redundancy throughout, especially with the prophets in the 'Old Testament' and the gospels in the 'New Testament'—surely one gospel could have sufficed?" Another common complaint regarded the manuscript's "often didactic, moralistic tone, an approach clearly unsuited to today's market." Another suggestion to consider, should you wish to revise the manuscript, concerns your use of sex and violence. Our readers were unanimous that today's reader would welcome a more generous and systematic yet judicious exploitation of these elements.

Our advice to you would be to consider more carefully current market tastes, should you wish to revise the manuscript. Also, we urge you to consider working with a professional editor, and with a literary agent who could offer you additional counsel in bringing your work to publishable levels.

Blessings on you as you seek to share your ideas through the written word,

Alan England
Senior editor—Non-fiction: Religion

50

A Pastor's Prayer for a Failing Body

*"The body is a unit, though it is made up of many
parts; and though all its parts are many, they form
one body. So it is with Christ."*

—1 CORINTHIANS 12:12

Lord, Woody Allen said "My main regret in life is that I'm not
someone else."
Well, I don't know about him, but could you make my church
someone else?

Lord, my church is in trouble.
We're just limping along.
We should be a church that runs and jumps.
Instead, we hobble and stumble.

We struggle merely to stand up straight;
When we do, it seems we hurt everywhere else.
We need knee replacement surgery.
And a couple of new hips.

Lord, you know how much old Mrs. Dodds annoys everyone:
With her whining, her sullen ingratitude, her perpetual
snippiness.
I don't know if she's a hip or a knee or some other part of your
body,
But if anyone is a candidate for a transplant, Lord, she is.

Her attitude contaminates us all, it seems.
So many in the church have a sour disposition.
We're not dealing with our body's toxicity as we should.
Would a kidney or liver transplant help?

And judging from the fights at our church council meetings,
I think we need a heart transplant too.
Or at least a few valve replacements.

Ours is a church that's so inward looking, Lord;
We see nothing beyond ourselves.
I fear we need a pair of cornea transplants.

The few visitors we get can see that our face no longer shows
    the beauty you gave us.
It is scarred from our fighting, our negativity, our nursing of
    grudges.
I know this is still pioneering medical technology, Lord,
But might you be able to arrange one of those face transplants?

Lord, this is far from a healthy body I'm trying to lead.
I think we may have we reached that point:
This body of believers needs a full-body transplant.

We need to be someone else.

But if that's too much to ask for,
Could you meanwhile give us
Some healthy, fully functional new body parts?
Please.

But if you can't do that either,
Could you at least create a new heart in me?